Pebble Plus

PEOPLE OF THE U.S. ARMED FORCES

SOLDIERS

OF THE U.S. ARMY

by Lisa M. Bolt Simons

Consulting Editor: Gail Saunders-Smith, PhD

Content Consultant: John Grady
Director of Communications, Association of the United States Army

Capstone
press

Mankato, Minnesota

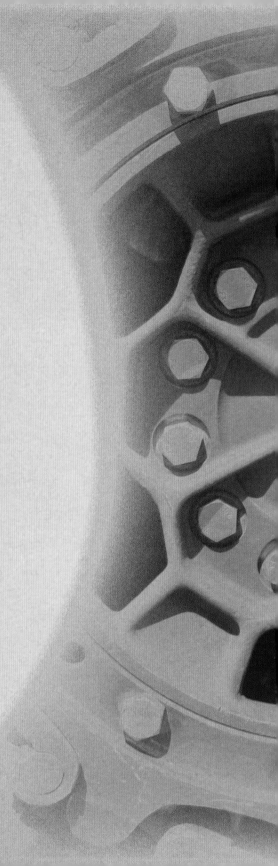

Pebble Plus is published by Capstone Press,
151 Good Counsel Drive, P.O. Box 669, Mankato, Minnesota 56002.
www.capstonepress.com

042010
005765

Library of Congress Cataloging-in-Publication Data
Simons, Lisa M. B., 1969 –
    Soldiers of the U.S. Army / by Lisa M. Bolt Simons.
    p. cm. — (Pebble plus. People of the U.S. Armed Forces)
    Includes bibliographical references and index.
    Summary: "A brief introduction to a soldier's life in the Army, including training, jobs, and life after service" — Provided by publisher.
    ISBN-13: 978-1-4296-2250-9 (hardcover)
    ISBN-13: 978-1-4296-5807-2 (saddle-stitched)
    1. United States. Army — Juvenile literature. I. Title.
UA25.S57 2009
355.3'30973 — dc22   2008026967

Editorial Credits
Gillia Olson, editor; Renée T. Doyle, designer; Jo Miller, photo researcher

Photo Credits
AP Images/Al Grillo, 15
Capstone Press/Gary Sundermeyer, 21
DoD photo by Senior Airman Steve Czyz, USAF, 17; Staff Sgt. Stacy L. Pearsall, USAF, 5
Photo Courtesy of Department of Defense, 19
Photo Courtesy of U.S. Army, 7, 9
Shutterstock/EchoArt, 1; risteski goce, 22–23
U.S. Air Force photo by Staff Sgt Jason T. Bailey, 13
U.S. Army photo by Staff Sgt Adam Mancin, cover
U.S. Navy photo by MC2 Sandra M. Palumbo, 11

Artistic Effects
Shutterstock/ariadna de raadt (tank tire), 2–3, 24
Shutterstock/Tamer Yazici (camouflage), cover, 1

Note to Parents and Teachers

The People of the U.S. Armed Forces series supports national science standards related to science, technology, and society. This book describes and illustrates soldiers of the U.S. Army. The images support early readers in understanding the text. The repetition of words and phrases helps early readers learn new words. This book also introduces early readers to subject-specific vocabulary words, which are defined in the Glossary section. Early readers may need assistance to read some words and to use the Table of Contents, Glossary, Read More, Internet Sites, and Index sections of the book.

Table of Contents

Joining the Army

Men and women join
the United States Army
to defend the country.
They protect the country
on land.

Recruits have basic training

for 10 weeks.

They exercise, march,

and learn to read maps.

They learn about weapons.

Job Training

After basic training,

recruits are called soldiers.

They learn new jobs.

Some drive Strykers, which

have armor to protect soldiers.

Infantry soldiers are trained
to fight on land.
They find their way with a
Global Positioning System (GPS).

Soldiers called engineers design and build bridges and roads.

Living on Post

Many soldiers live
in places called posts.
Posts have homes,
restaurants, and stores
for soldiers and their families.

Posts are

in the United States

or other countries.

A soldier changes posts

every three to four years.

Serving the Country

Most Army soldiers serve

two to six years.

Some soldiers serve

20 years or more.

The Army is their career.

Soldiers who leave the Army

are called civilians.

Some find jobs.

Others go to college.

Glossary

basic training — the first training period for people who join the military

career — the type of work a person does

civilian — a person who is not in the military

infantry — a group of people in the military trained to fight on land

post — an area run by the military where people serving in the military live and military supplies are stored

recruit — a person who has just joined the military

Stryker — an armored vehicle; Strykers look like tanks, but they have wheels rather than tracks.

weapon — an object used to protect or attack; a gun is a weapon.

Read More

Braulick, Carrie A. *U.S. Army Tanks.* Military Vehicles. Mankato, Minn.: Capstone Press, 2006.

Doeden, Matt. *The U.S. Army.* Military Branches. Mankato, Minn.: Capstone Press, 2009.

Hamilton, John. *The Army.* Defending the Nation. Edina, Minn.: Abdo, 2007.

Internet Sites

FactHound offers a safe, fun way to find educator-approved Internet sites related to this book.

Here's what you do:

1. Visit *www.facthound.com*
2. Choose your grade level.
3. Begin your search.

This book's ID number is 9781429622509.

FactHound will fetch the best sites for you!

23

Index

Word Count: 155
Grade: 1
Early-Intervention Level: 22